Herobrine Goes on Vacation

Zack Zombie Books

Chapter 1
The Announcement

"We're all going to Hawaii for vacation!"

The news Mr. Lurker delivered at the dinner table came as a big surprise. I had never heard of Hawaii before. But when Mr. Lurker explained that it was a land full of volcanos and nuts, it sounded a lot like home.

Lucy was the first to groan.

"I thought you loved Hawaii," replied Mrs. Lurker before turning to her husband. "Oh, I'm so excited. We haven't been to Hawaii in years."

Mr. and Mrs. Lurker got up from the table and made coffee as Lucy and I cleared the plates.

"So, Herobrine," Lucy said as she started to wash the dishes, "this'll be your first vacation?"

I nodded as I took the plate from her hand. I didn't really know what to do with it, so I just put it back in the sink when Lucy wasn't looking.

"You have no idea what a vacation is, do you?" she continued.

"Err, not really," I said.

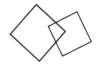

"Don't worry," chuckled Lucy. "I'll teach you all about it."

It took a really long time to do the dishes. But, once we finished, Lucy and I headed to her Dad's office and fired up the computer.

Mr. Lurker's computer was the oldest computer I had ever seen. He had bought it ten years ago and had refused to get a new one. Lucy's computer was getting fixed, so it was the only one we had.

The computer monitor was really big. It looked a lot like my cousin. At least from the side.

The keyboard was yellow with brown and green crust on each of the keys. Kinda looked like somebody sneezed on it and then left it out in the sunlight to let it bake until golden brown.

Lucy looked at it and almost gagged, especially when I started to scratch the keys so I could spell my name.

After about five minutes of scraping, and a lot of clunking and whirring, the computer came to life.

"Here we go," she said, trying really hard to not touch the keys with her bare hands.

Then she typed a few words on the keyboard.

"See, it says here that a vacation is all about taking a break to relax and have fun."

"You mean like this?"

POP!

Lucy looked at me with that confused look she gives me sometimes. I think she was just jealous she couldn't take her head off like that.

POP! There, good as new.

"Anyway, a vacation is supposed to be a time when you throw your head back, relax and do things that are a lot of fun."

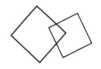

I gave Lucy a confused look. "Isn't that what I just. . .?"

"Fun. . .You know, things that make you happy. What's something that makes you happy, Herobrine?"

"Uh. . .I'm really happy that I can talk and burp at the same time. Like this. . . RRRRRRUUCCCYRRRRUUURRKKERR!!!"

"What was that?!!!!" Lucy's dad yelled from upstairs.

"Nothing, Dad! It was just. . .uh. . .the neighbors mowing their lawn."

"At eight o'clock at night?" Mr. Lurker said. "Wow, those Hendersons must really love their lawn."

"I'm also really happy that I can burp and fart at the same time, too," I said. "Like this. . ."

"That's OK!" Lucy said, abruptly ending our vacation lesson.

Lucy awkwardly shut the computer down with her foot because she got tired of using her elbows. And then we headed to our bedrooms.

When I went into my room, Mr. Lurker came in and gave me something called a SOOT-CASE. I smiled and acted like I knew what it was.

After Mr. Lurker left, I tried to figure out how to use it.

After a few minutes of fidgeting with it, I finally figured out what a SOOT-CASE is for. It took me a few tries, but I finally got it on.

Fit like a glove.

I was hard getting the zipper all the way around my head, though. But I finally got it.

The only problem was that I couldn't see.

Well, this is easy. I'll just make some eyeholes.

Making eyeholes was easy for a guy with heat vision.

ZZZT – BOOMM!!!!

PSSSSTTTT!

"What in tarnation was that?!!!!!" I heard Lucy's dad yell.

Lucy ran into my room and then ran into the bathroom. She turned something that made all the steam stop from shooting all over the place.

She gave me that look again.

"Whardoyouthurk?!!!" I asked Lucy.

"What? I can't hear you Herobrine."

"Irrsar Whardoyouthurk?!!"

"What?!!!"

Then she unzipped my new hat and took it off my head.

"Hey, what did you do that for? I liked that hat."

Again, the weird look.

Anyway, Lucy took the soot-case and started to put things in it. I knew humans were weird, so I didn't even try to figure out why she was doing it.

So, I started to throw some things into it too.

"What in the world are you doing?" Lucy asked.

"Uh. . .vacation?" I replied, acting like it was obvious.

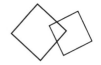

"You don't need all of that," she said as she pulled the bed pan out of the soot-case.

"Listen, just put some T-shirts and jeans in it and you'll be OK."

So, I did just that. I put some of my turquoise T-shirts and blue jeans in the hat, and I lifted it up, but it was heavier than before. Not to mention it was even harder to put over my head.

Lucy just took her hand and smacked herself in the forehead with it. I think that meant she was constipated. So, I just left her alone in my room to do her duty.

I went over to help Mr. and Mrs. Lurker with their soot-cases. But every time I lifted it up over Mr. Lurker's head, he got mad at me and started saying strange words to himself.

Finally, Mrs. Lurker just took me to the kitchen to give me some cookies.

As soon as Mr. Lurker came down, he came to the kitchen.

"Got the tickets, dear?" Mrs. Lurker asked Mr. Lurker.

"Yes," replied Mr. Lurker, pulling four airline tickets from his chest pocket. "Two adults, one child and. . ."

Mr. Lurker paused and looked at me.

"I didn't know which box to check for you, Herobrine. I wasn't sure if you qualify as a child or a second carry on. So, I just selected 'other.' He. He."

I didn't really know what that meant. But I was just glad that we were going on an ARROW-PLANE. I heard about those from Lucy. Though, I didn't really understand how they got it to fly with all those people on it.

Man, the bow must be huge.

Mrs. Lurker asked me, "Herobrine, are you excited?"

"Yes! I'm so excited I could blow something up!" I cried.

Mr. and Mrs. Lurker just stood there and stared at me.

"Yes, dear. Well, maybe just don't say that out loud in the airport, OK?" replied Mrs. Lurker. "How about another cookie?"

Chapter 2
The Airport

I stood at the entrance to the ARROW-PORT as they launched an ARROW-PLANE into the sky. . .so awesome.

"Come on, Herobrine, or you'll be standing here all day," Mr. Lurker said. "Do you want to just watch the planes or fly in one?"

Then Mr. Lurker walked in through some invisible doors. They just opened all by themselves and sucked him in.

Whoa! An invisible portal, I thought.

I was really weirded out by how Mr. Lurker just walked through the portal like that. But Mr. Lurker kept waving his arms like he really wanted me to go through it.

So, I closed my eyes and jumped through.

WHAM!

OW!

WHAM!

OW!

WHAM!

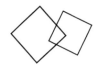

OW!

WHAM!

OW!

For some reason, the portal wouldn't open for me.

Then Mr. Lurker popped his head out of the portal.

"Herobrine, get in here! We're gonna be late!"

I saw his head pop back into the portal, and I jumped after it.

WHAM!

OW!

After about ten or fifteen tries, I finally got through but not without the help of a big guy in a blue uniform. I think he said the portal couldn't tell if I was human or cargo.

Whatever. All I know is that the shape of my head was a lot different than when I first got to the airport.

Now the airport was full of people dragging soot-cases all around the arrow-port. Kinda reminded me of home. . .but without the Endermen.

I raced Lucy to what looked like a table with a lady behind it.

"Good evening and welcome to U-Wizz Airways. My name is Lucinda. How can I help you on this fine day?"

Mr. Lurker took out the tickets and passed them to Lucinda. She smiled at Mr. Lurker and Mrs. Lurker. But when she saw me next to Lucy she gave her a strange look.

Yeah, Lucy can creep people out sometimes. She's had that effect on people ever since I first met her. So I'm used to the weird looks we get when we're together in public.

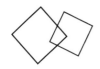

"All okay?" Mr. Lurker said.

"Hold on one minute please, sir," Lucinda replied before picking up a phone and launching her voice over the arrow-port.

"Could a member of security please attend desk 14. That's a member of security to desk 14. Code 7."

Mr. Lurker just took his hand and slapped himself on the forehead.

Wow. Constipation must run in Lucy's family.

So, I opened my soot-case and put it behind Mr. Lurker in case he needed some backup.

Then I felt a big, meaty hand trying to grab my shoulder.

"Is this the one?" the heavily set security officer said, giving me and Lucy a strange look.

Poor Lucy. I think I'm her only friend.

Lucinda nodded and handed him my ticket.

"Okay. Can you come with me?" he said, turning me around. "Whoa!" he said as my eyes glowed brightly in his face.

"Everything all right?" Mr. Lurker questioned.

"This. . .err. . .passenger just needs to go through some extra security with me. Shouldn't take long. You go through to the gate, sir," the security officer said to Mr. Lurker.

"You come with me," he grunted.

He tried to get hold of my arm, but he couldn't get his fat fingers around it. So he just pointed where he wanted me to go.

After we went to the side, he started to ask me questions.

"Excuse me. . .uh. . .sir, I just have to ask you a few questions."

He pulled a pen from his pocket and clicked the end.

"What would you. . .uh. . .call yourself?"

"Herobrine," I said.

"No, I mean what are you? Like what species?"

"I'm a Mob," I said.

"YOU"RE WITH THE MOB?!!! he said as he quickly grabbed hold of his side.

He must have a tummy ache, I thought.

"I'm Herobrine, from a place called the Nether. It's kinda hot. . .like Hawaii."

He just gave me a blank look.

"It's in Minecraft."

"AIRCRAFT?!!!" WHAT ABOUT THE AIRCRAFT?!!!" he said, grabbing his side again.

"No Minecraft," I said.

"Minecraft? Where is that?"

"In the Overworld," I said.

"YOUR GOING TO TAKE OVER THE WORLD?!!" he said, grabbing his side really tight this time.

I went over to him and rubbed his belly a little bit. I saw Mrs. Lurker do that to Lucy when she got the bubble guts.

"Okay, let's just cut to the chase," he said as he shoved my hand off his belly. "I don't want to hold you up any longer than I have to. We have a lot more people here wanting to get on with their vacations."

Ohhhhh, vacation. That's it.

So, I showed him that I can vacation really good.

POP!

He just stared at me, not knowing what to write down on his little note pad.

"Uh. . .you can go," he said.

So, I ran as fast as I could toward the metal blinking portal that everyone was teleporting through.

"Woah! Slow down," said the man sitting on the side. "Arms by your side please and walk through."

I didn't want to miss Lucy and her parents, so I did as he said. I stepped forward through the portal. . .and then. . .

BEEP! BEEP! BEEP!

My body got stuck inside. The alarm sounded as half a dozen men and women came charging toward me.

I heard a loud voice say that the arrow-plane to Hawaii was leaving soon.

Oh, man! I was going to miss my trip!

Chapter 3
The Flight

It took about fifteen security people, but I finally got through the portal. I know because everyone was saying how the portal was made for people not cargo. . .whatever that meant.

Man, humans are so weird.

When I finally got to the next desk, a short, round woman with a small moustache quickly scanned my ticket. No alarm sounded, so I ran to the plane.

I got to the arrow-plane gate just in time. The lady at the front desk gave me a strange look as she put her hand over her mouth.

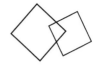

She called the guys carrying all the luggage to come help me get on board.

But then Lucy came out.

"There you are, Herobrine. Why are you taking so long?"

She walked onto the plane, and as I followed behind her I banged my head on the door.

Then we had to walk down a weird aisle with a bunch of people sitting on each side.

"Watch it!" one woman cried as she accidentally hit my fist with her head.

"Sit down!" came another angry passenger who hit my elbow with his face.

"Hey, be careful!" another lady yelled. But I didn't understand why. The way she stuck her foot out, I thought she wanted me to stand on it.

"Move your luggage!" a man said to Lucy as she tried to lead me to my seat.

I could see Mr. Lurker looking at us and shaking his head. Lucy hung her head low too. But, I think she was just sad everyone was yelling at her for being so clumsy.

I eventually made my way to two seats in the back and sat down. The two seats were really comfortable, and they were a perfect fit for my square butt.

Suddenly, people started talking over the speaker. When they were finished, the lights turned off.

"Switch that bright light off, will you?" shouted a man in the seat in front of me. When he turned around, he gave me a panicked look and then faced forward again.

"No one seem very happy with their vacation," I whispered to Lucy.

Lucy just rolled her eyes and put on her headphones.

A few hours later, we finally arrived in Hawaii. The moment the doors were opened, everybody rushed off as fast as they could. All they kept talking about was all their bruises.

Man, humans are so weird.

Then Mr. and Mrs. Lurker and Lucy left the plane without me.

But, when I tried to get up, I couldn't. I think I was stuck.

It took the entire crew to help me out of the seats. I think my butt didn't really want to leave.

Man, those seats were comfortable.

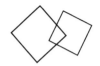

As I stepped down the aisle, I passed the people in uniform.

"Happy vacation," I said.

POP!

The flight attendants didn't say a word, they just gave me a look like they were really happy to get me off the plane and help me start my vacation.

Chapter 4
The Welcome

"Ah! There's our ride!" Mr. Lurker announced, seeing a big white bus coming toward us.

After a short drive, we arrived at a big building with huge, hairy trees. I think Lucy called it the Kiki Hotel. Or did she say Freaky Hotel?

Can't remember. But after seeing the hairy trees, the hairy fruit and the hairy people in tank tops and sandals, the Freaky Hotel made a lot more sense.

We took the elevator up to our rooms. Mr.
and Mrs. Lurker went into their room and
Lucy went to her room. I went to Lucy's room
too, but she told me I had my own room and
pointed to the door next to hers.

I tried to get in my room, but for some reason,
the door just wouldn't open.

BAM!

OW!

BAM!

OW!

BAM!

OW!

Lucy heard all the banging, so she came out to help me. And for some reason, the door just opened for Lucy, really easy.

Yeah, I think Lucy's a witch.

Lucy came into my room to help me unpack. But, when I opened my soot-case, my shirt looked like somebody threw up on it a few times.

"Eww! Somebody ralphed on my shirt!" I said.

"That's supposed to be like that," Lucy said. "It's called a Hawaiian shirt. Everybody in Hawaii wears those."

Wait a minute. . .I thought. People actually ralph on each other and then wear it around for everyone to see?

Well, I guess if I'm going to be in Hawaii, I might as well act like a Hawaiian.

"BBBBLLEEEECCCHH!"

SPLATTT!

"AAAAAAAHHHHH!!!!!"

All of a sudden, Lucy ran to her room.

Wow. She's excited, I thought.

She probably can't wait to see what it's gonna look like when it dries.

I looked at the red and orange shirt in my hands. Now that I was in Hawaii I might as well dress like a Hawaiian. So, I took off my clothes and put it on.

Lucy said we were all going swimming later and that I should bring a towel. So, I grabbed one from the bathroom and headed downstairs.

Now that I think of it, I have never gone swimming in the human world before...

Can't wait.

I took the elevator right down to the ground floor. I asked around for where the swimming area was, but nobody seemed to want to talk to me.

They just gave me weird looks.

Maybe my shirt wasn't fully dry yet.

I finally found the swimming area and it looked like a huge lake in the shape of a giant kidney bean. A group of small kids were playing with a ball in the water. They were knocking it up in the air to one another and laughing as they played.

It looked like fun so I walked into the water to play with them. Suddenly, the beach ball got knocked in my direction. It was heading straight for me so I stepped forward to hit the ball back.

POW!

PSSSSS…

All of a sudden, the kids began to cry. Their father looked at me with a really mean look, so I decided to catch up with Lucy and her parents as quickly as I could.

As I got up out of the pool, I saw Mr. and Mrs. Lurker coming toward the swimming area, and I waved to them.

"AAAAAAAAHHH!" Mrs. Lurker screamed.

"What in tarnation?!!!" Mr. Lurker said, grabbing a towel and putting it around my waist.

"Boy, didn't you pack any underwear?!!!"

"Yes, it's upstairs," I said. "How do you like my shirt?"

Chapter 5
The Beach

We got to the beach just a little after lunch. The beach was curved and all around it were these plastic white chairs. I helped Mr. Lurker find a few, and we dragged them across the beach so that we had four of them together.

Mr. and Mrs. Lurker pulled out a bottle of what looked like mayonnaise and started to put it on themselves. Lucy did the same.

And I thought wearing underwear in public was weird. . .What did Lucy call them, again? Speedos. . .so weird.

Now, I had never seen people put on mayo before, but we were in Hawaii so I decided to give it a go. I grabbed a bottle of mayonnaise from the food bag and took off the Hawaiian shirt. Then I squirted some mayo into my hands and tried rubbing it over my body like Lucy did.

For some reason, it didn't stick to me like it did on Lucy. The mayo just glided right over my body. I thought I had made a mistake and picked up the butter instead.

I tried and tried to rub it in like Lucy did, but it was no use. I eventually gave up and laid down on the plastic chair.

But as soon as I laid down, I just slid off the end of the chair and onto the sand.

Squeeeeeaal! Flump!

Squeeeeeaal! Flump!

Squeeeeeeaaaaaeeeeeaaaaalllleeeeaaaaaalllll! Flump!

After about fifteen tries, I finally gave up.

As I stood up, a little kid came up to me and asked me if I sell ice cream. He said I looked like a toasted almond bar.

Somebody else came up to me and asked me if I sell corn dogs. As I looked around all I could see other people were starting to walk toward me with money in their hands.

It was all kinda weird, so I decided to go for a walk. There was a quieter section of the beach at the far end of the cove, so I just walked over to take a break from all the drama.

Chapter 6
The Idol

After a while, I sat down on one of the large rocks and looked out at the ocean. I was starting to think how weird this vacation stuff was when something caught my eye. Near the water, sticking out of the sand, there was an object.

I jumped down from the rock and slowly walked toward it. I looked around. There was no one around except for one guy who looked like one of the islanders floating on a big door.

Man, humans are so weird.

I bent down and looked at the object more closely. Then I reached down and pulled it from the sand.

The object was carved from stone and was about the size of my hand. It looked like a little guy with a big head, and a really big mouth that looked like it was screaming, laughing or had really bad case of explosive diarrhea.

As I held it, I felt a weird vibe run through me.

It felt kinda like when I put my head in the microwave at Lucy's house once. It thought it was a good idea at the time. I mean, I was a little cold, and it looked so square and all. . ."

BOOF!

Suddenly, something hit me in the back of the head and knocked me to the ground.

"Hey, dude! I wouldn't keep that if I was you!"

It was the guy on the big door. He had chased after me, only to accidentally knock me down with his big door.

"Ow," I said rubbing my head. "Is it yours?" I asked, holding it out toward him.

The guy jumped back really fast. "No way, man. Not mine. I wouldn't take that if you gave me a million bucks."

"Really? Why not?"

"The thing's Taboo, dude!" the guy kept saying, keeping his distance.

"Tab-who?" I asked him.

"Taboo. It's an ancient idol known as a Taboo Tiki. Bad things happen to whoever touches it, man. That thing'll bring you bad luck."

I had a feeling this guy was trying to trick me and really wanted it for himself. But I wanted to keep it. The statue kinda reminded me of Mr. Lurker. . .especially when he's on the toilet.

"Naw. I think I'm gonna keep it," I said.

"You're crazy, dude. But, don't say I didn't warn you."

The islander wandered off, slicking back his hair and shaking his head as he turned and walked away. . .

BOOF!

. . .And smacked me in the face with his door again.

Ow.

With the guy gone, I decided to stroll back to rejoin the Lurkers.

As we packed up our things and headed back to the Freaky Hotel to prepare for dinner, I started thinking about what the islander with the big door had said.

Bad luck? Me? That could never happen.

Everything always goes my way.

So, I took a string and put it through the two holes on top of the Tiki idol.

This will make a great souvenir, I thought as I put it on.

Chapter 7
The Magician

After dinner, we went over to the information table. There was a lady there who read off a list of activities we could do for fun. There was something called SNORE-KILLING, SCOOBY-DIVING, BUN-JEE JUMPING, and something called MOOLA DANCING (which I think is when people throw money at you when you dance). . .but the list went on and on.

"Okay, Herobrine," Mrs. Lurker said, "what would you like to do? You can choose first."

The only thing I understood was the volcano tour. A volcano sounded a lot like home, and I could really use something normal right now.

"I want to try the volcano tour."

"Oh! I'm up for the volcano tour, too." Lucy said really excited.

Mrs. Lurker laughed. "Good idea you two. What else shall we do, darling?"

Mr. Lurker looked at the list. I was sure he would choose SNORE-KILLING.

"How about hula dancing?" Mrs. Lurker suggested.

After Mrs. Lurker said that, Mr. Lurker's face looked just like the Tiki's.

"Dancing, really?

"Yes, it'll be fun!" Mrs. Lurker continued.

"Well, okay. If that's what you want."

Mrs. Lurker went over to the information desk and booked us in for MOOLA DANCING and a volcano tour. I was really looking forward to the volcano tour more, though. I don't think my speedos have any pockets to put money into.

After, we headed to some place called the HE-ATE-HER. Or something like that.

Anyway, inside was a stage and a lot of round tables everywhere. The show looked like it was about to start and the only table available was one right in the center at the front.

We all went to the table and sat down. All of a sudden, all the lights turned off and a big light started shining on the stage.

And no. . .it wasn't me.

Then the curtain on the stage opened.

"Hello, welcome and good evening to you all," said the man as he strode on stage in a really big hat and black cape. "My name is Sirius Squarebottom the Sorcerer!"

"PFFFFT! What kind of name is that?" Lucy whispered in my ear with a giggle.

I don't know. I kinda liked it.

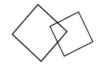

"Tonight, I shall be bringing you the finest magic tricks that Hawaii has to offer, but first I need a volunteer."

A light suddenly shined into the audience. The light hovered around for a little while and then it ended up on me.

"Ah! A prefect assistant for a perfect night of magic!"

Before I knew it, I was being helped up from my seat by two women and taken up onto the stage. I had hardly blinked and I was standing beside the magician with everyone staring at me.

"Very well!" he announced. "Let the magic begin!"

The magician stepped to the side of the stage and took me with him. He removed his cape as the two ladies wheeled out a long, horizontal box.

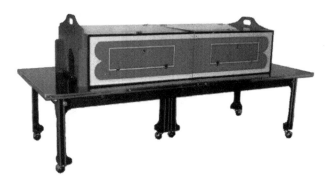

"What is your name?"

"Herobrine!"

"Herbyline! Perfect. Will you lie down inside this box, please?"

I looked at Lucy, not really sure if I should trust this guy.

"Lie down, please, Herbyline!"

I stepped toward the box and the ladies helped me to lie down inside it. They then closed the covers, locked me in, and spun the entire thing round several times really fast. By the time they stopped, all my dinner started working its way back though my system. I could've made like five Hawaiian shirts after all that spinning.

"Now ladies and gentlemen, be amazed as I saw Herbyline in half!"

What the what?!!!

I started to wriggle and try to get out, but I couldn't move. That box was locked. Only my head was sticking out one end of the box, the rest of me was in the box as the magician took a saw and put it on the top of the box.

"Now, boys and girls, remember this is only a magic trick so please, please do not try this at home."

Then, Sirius Squarebottom the Sorcerer took the saw and sawed the box and me in half!

The two ladies each pulled an end and the box, and my body split in two!

I almost fainted and started thinking that if they find my corpse, it's probably not going to smell very good.

After a few minutes, the ladies put the box back together. Then they undid the lid and told me to come out.

When I came out, the ladies gave me a look that made me think that, yeah, they knew it was me.

But, honestly, I didn't care. I was just glad I was still alive.

I wanted to make sure everything was still working so...

POP!

All of a sudden, everybody started yelling and screaming and running out of the place.

I looked over at Lucy and Mr. and Mrs. Lurker. Mr. Lurker just took his hand and smacked himself on the forehead.

So did Lucy.

After all the commotion, all I wanted to do was get back to the hotel room. So, we made our way back to the elevator and back to our rooms.

I was really tired, so I took the Tiki idol off and put it on the stand and went to bed.

But, that night, I had the weirdest dream. I don't usually dream, but once I was asleep I had a dream that the Taboo Tiki started talking to me. He said his name was Melvin and that he's gotten a bum rap. He said he's actually a good luck charm, but the dummies that carry him around are just clumsy, that's all. Then Melvin said that it wasn't a big deal since the whole island was going to be destroyed anyway.

What the what?!!!

All of a sudden, I woke up and I looked over at Melvin.

You know, he didn't seem like a Melvin to me. . .More like a Damien. . .or a Chucky.

Then I went back to sleep, as I stared at the big creepy grin on Melvin's face.

Chapter 8
The Dance

The next evening, we all went with Mrs. Lurker to learn how to dance like Hawaiians do.

"Welcome, everyone!" the dance instructor said. "My name is Alani, and tonight I shall be teaching you the famous Hawaii hula dance."

The dance instructor had on a brown grass skirt that seemed like it wasn't meant for somebody with a belly like hers.

"Now, everyone, collect a hula hoop from over there please. I'm going to start with the basics to help you master our wonderful dance."

Mr. and Mrs. Lurker, and me and Lucy went and took a big circle thing and found some room on the grass in front of the instructor.

"Now, a hula dance is all in the hips. If you master that, you are close to mastering the hula."

I looked down at my waist. Yeah, somebody stole my hips.

The instructor started swirling her butt around and told us to copy her. I held my hoop for a moment and watched as Lucy gave it a try. She had obviously done this before. Mrs. Lurker

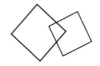

was the same. Not quite as good, but she had the general idea.

Poor Mr. Lurker. It looked like someone stole his hips too.

I stepped into the hoop and pulled it up to where my hips should have been. Then the hoop just dropped to the floor. After about ten tries, I finally got the hoop to spin around me.

Since I had no hips, the hoop started moving up to my chest. My hands were over my head, and suddenly I was spinning so fast the hula hoop shot up over my head and flew off into the air. It hurtled toward the eating area, got caught on a rotating ceiling fan and shot back to where we were, hitting the instructor right in the face. She threw her hand over her mouth and ran away.

Everyone else stopped their spinning and stared straight at me.

All I could do was shrug in embarrassment.

But honestly, I was just thinking about how lucky I was that the hoop didn't come back and hit me in the face.

Wow, Melvin is already starting to bring me luck, I thought.

So cool.

Chapter 9
The Charm

We woke up extra early because today we were going on our volcano tour.

I got dressed and got ready to join the Lurkers in something called the BOO-FAY room for breakfast. But, when I was about to leave my room, I realized I had almost forgot to bring my new good luck charm.

So, I threw Melvin over my head and made my way down to breakfast.

Unfortunately, this was the morning the elevator decided to stop working. There was a big sign next to it that said:

ELEVATOR BROKEN. PLEASE USE THE STAIRS.

So, I ran down the stairs so I wouldn't be late.

Except, I don't know if it was that the stairs were made of marble or that my feet were so flat, but as soon as my foot touched the first stair...

BUMP! BAM! BUMP! BAM! BAM! BUMP! BUMP! BAM! BUMP! ...

SQUISH!

It's a good thing a really big, blubbery Hawaiian guy was coming up the stairs.

When I cleaned myself off, I didn't even have a scratch.

Thanks, Melvin, I thought as I gave him a quick pat on the head.

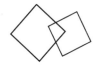

"Hello, Herobrine," Mrs. Lurker said as she, Mr. Lurker, and Lucy walked into the boo-fay room.

"That was really interesting dancing last night, eh, Herobrine?" Mr. Lurker asked.

I didn't know what to say. I didn't plan to hit someone in the face with a flying hula hoop. I was just glad it wasn't me getting hit in the face.

Thanks to Melvin, I thought.

We finished our breakfast, then headed to the front of the hotel to wait for our bus.

The bus we got on was really small, which Mr. Lurker really didn't like. Especially since the driver's dog was sitting in the best seat.

"How can people drive a thing like this?" Mr. Lurker said, getting on the bus. "It's a glorified can!"

After a little while of driving, Mr. Lurker got quiet. So, we all just figured he fell asleep.

"What's that?" Lucy asked me pointing to my new good luck charm.

"Oh, this is Melvin. He's my good luck charm," I said proudly.

"You don't really believe in that stuff, do you?" Lucy said, giggling at me.

"Well, it's sure kept me out of some really bad situations these past few days," I said.

"Let me see that," Lucy said, putting out her hand.

So, I took Melvin off and handed him to her.

"Oh, Melvin, bring me a million dollars right now," Lucy said sarcastically as she held Melvin to her chest.

After waiting a few seconds, Lucy said, "See. Nothing. So, lame, Herobrine."

Suddenly, the dog stuck his head out the window and started barking.

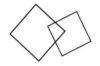

Lucy and I both stuck our heads out of the bus window to see what all the commotion is about.

"It's just a bird," Mrs. Lurker said

But me and Lucy just started having fun copying the dog as he stuck his head out of the bus and let his tongue hang out.

First I did it, then Lucy did it.

"Look at those pretty birds," Mrs. Lurker said, looking up.

PLOP!

Next thing I know, a glob of something white and slimy landed on my shirt.

"Ewww!" I said.

"Ha! Some good luck charm," Lucy said, laughing out loud and acting like the dog.

PLOP! PLOP!

That is, until she got hit with some slime.

Except it didn't land on her shirt.

Let's just say, we're probably not going to be sticking our tongues out of the car window anymore.

Chapter 10
The Store

When we arrived at Volcano Park, Lucy ran to the bathroom to clean up.

I was just lucky that I only got hit on the shoulder.

Lucy, not so much.

Man, Melvin is just the best lucky charm ever, I thought.

I threw on my backpack and we strode over to a collection of huts that explained all about volcanoes. Looking at the pictures of the flowing lava reminded me of back home.

Ah, there's no place like the Nether, I thought.

We headed outside and looked at the steam vents that were all around. Mr. Lurker decided to get his camera out to take some pictures.

We headed to some railings that provided the perfect lookout point to see the volcano. The volcano looked amazing.

But the tour guide said that the volcano looked even more impressive at night.

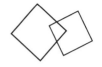

"Shall we stick around to see the volcano tonight?" Mrs. Lurker asked.

"You know, honey," Mr Lurker said with a smile, "that's exactly what I was thinking."

We all got back into the cramped bus and headed to the nearest town to do some more sightseeing and get something to eat.

The nearest town wasn't far away. It was a small place, but had some stores and a restaurant.

We wandered to a place called the Volcanic Store. When we went in, a device in the door gave a small eruption noise.

"Whoo, excuse me," I said, waving my hand.

Lucy thought it was funny. But Mr. Lurker just rolled his eyes.

As we entered, a small, old Hawaiian man came out from the back room and stood behind the counter.

"A volcanic welcome to my humble store," the man said. He moved onto a small set of steps so we could see him better. "Can I help you with anything specific?"

"No, not really," Mr. Lurker said. "Just browsing."

The man gave Lucy and me a strange look.

I went over to him and let him know that I understood. Lucy is just special, that's all.

The man then looked at Melvin around my neck, and suddenly turned white.

"It shouldn't be here," the man cried, jumping down from the steps and scuttling round to the front of the counter.

"Hey! She's different, I know, but she has as much right to be here as you and me!" I said, jumping to Lucy's defense.

"Get out! Get away from this place! We don't want you around here!"

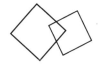

The man ushered us to the door, pushed us through it, and slammed it behind us.

"Huh! Weird guy!" said Mrs. Lurker. "Any idea what that was about, Herobrine?"

"No!" I said, patting Lucy's hand to make her feel better. "No idea at all."

Chapter 11
The Restaurant

We wandered around the small town for the rest of the day and then headed into the local restaurant.

When we finished eating, Mr. Lurker wanted to make toast. I didn't understand why, since we were all really full.

"I want to make a toast," Mr. Lurker said, "here's to a great vacation."

Then everybody raised their glasses. I didn't see any toast, though.

Like I said. . .humans. . .weird.

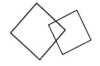

Next thing, they jammed their glasses together. I didn't want to be left out so I did it too.

KRESH!

"Herobrine! What did you do that for?!!" Mr. Lurker yelled.

"Uh. . .toast?"

They all gave me that look again.

"Well, it's a good thing you didn't get cut," Mrs. Lurker said.

Thanks, Melvin, I thought as I stooped under the table to pick up the broken pieces.

BUMP!

"OW!" I said after bumping my head on the table.

All the plates that were on the table fell on the floor.

So, we started to pick everything up.

I was about to pick up the salt shaker, when all of a sudden a waiter's foot came out of nowhere.

Next thing I know, the waiter's legs were up in the air.

"BLAM! SPLAT!"

"OW!"

"EWW!"

I got hit with the big metal plate he was carrying and then I got covered in all the food that was on it.

So, I got up to go clean up in the bathroom.

BABBABLAM-KRESH!!!!

Right when I got up, the light thingy came crashing down right on the chair I was sitting on.

"Herobrine, you are so lucky you weren't sitting down!" Mrs. Lurker said.

Wow. She's right. I am lucky. But it's all thanks to Melvin, I thought as I picked him up and looked at him.

Melvin's creepy smile looked bigger and creepier than usual.

But, eh. . .I'm just happy he's been keeping me out of so much trouble.

Chapter 12
The Old Man

As we made our way through the town, I saw the old man from the shop again. He looked like he was following us.

"PSSST!" the old man said to me. "Come here. I have something important to tell you."

"Uh. . .me and Lucy are going to get some ice cream," I said to Mr. and Mrs. Lurker. We'll catch up with you later."

"That sounds great," Mr. Lurker said, getting surprisingly happy.

So, I grabbed Lucy's arm and walked around the corner to where the old man was.

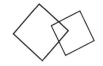

"Herobrine, what are you up to now?" Lucy asked.

"It's the old man from the store," I said as we walked around the corner.

As we met up with the old man, he was out of breath because it looked like he was running all over the place trying to find us.

"Hey. . .wheeze. . .you're. . .wheeze. . .in. . . wheeze. . .a. . .wheeze. . .lot. . .wheeze. . . of. . . wheeze. . .cough. . .wheeze. . .cough, cough. . ."

"What is it?!! Lucy said, frantic because it sounded serious.

After the old man caught his breath, he finished what he had to say.

"I said, you're in a lot of trouble. That idol is Taboo," he finally spit out.

"Yeah, it's my Taboo Tiki," I said. "His name is Melvin, and he's my good luck charm."

"No. . .it is Taboo. . .That means bad things will happen to whoever has it," he said.

"No way," I said. "If it wasn't for Melvin, I would've been hit in the face with a hula hoop. And if it wasn't for Melvin, there wouldn't have been a fat Hawaiian guy to break my fall when I fell down the stairs. And if it wasn't for Melvin, I would've gotten cut when I broke the glass when Mr. Lurker made toast. And if it wasn't for Melvin, I would have been squished when the light thingy fell on my chair."

Lucy and the old man just stared at me.

"What?"

Then Lucy raised an eyebrow.

"Ohhhhhhh. You mean when the hoop hit the. . .and I fell down the. . .and the glass broke when I. . .and the light thingy fell down on the. . .Ohhhhhhh."

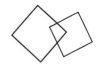

Then Lucy chimed in. "Wait a minute. . .I was holding that thing when those birds dropped the. . ."

"Ooooooh, sssssss, yeah. . .sorry about that," I said.

"So, how do we get rid of it?" Lucy asked the old man.

"You cannot," he said. "Once you have picked it up, the Taboo stays with you forever."

"No way!" I said. Then I took Melvin off and threw him as far from me as I could.

Next thing I know, Melvin hit a bird and then the bird fell on a car, which cracked the windshield, which made the car swerve and hit a fire hydrant, which splashed on a dog, which got so scared it took off, which dragged his owner down the street, which made the owner trip and fall on a table that Melvin had landed on, which threw Melvin up into the air and. . .

BUMP!

OW!

Melvin hit me right on my head.

"See, Taboo stays with you forever," the old man said.

"But, there's gotta be a way to get rid of Melvin!" I said frantically as I looked at Melvin's enormous creepy smile.

"There is one way, but it is very dangerous," the old man said. "You must throw the idol into the mouth of a volcano."

Then Lucy and I turned around and looked at the huge volcano that was behind us.

"OK. Gulp. If that's what it takes, let's do it," I said.

Chapter 13
The Volcano

In the evening, we took the bus and headed up to the lookout point near the top of the volcano.

The Lurkers and I stood there for some time taking in the view. Mr. Lurker put his arms around his wife. Lucy and I just looked at each other, and we knew what we had to do.

As Mr. and Mrs. Lurker turned and headed inside to get a warm drink, me and Lucy grabbed our chance. I took Melvin out of my pocket. He was still a little wet and brown.

Yeah, I tried to flush him down the toilet, but it didn't work out too well.

I held Melvin in the palm of my hand and looked at him one final time. His creepy smile was bigger than ever. Almost like he knew something that we didn't.

Then, Lucy and I glanced around. There weren't many people around now. So with no one to see us, I sneaked under the railings and onto the surface of the volcano.

I crouched as low as I could to the ground and made my way as close to the opening of the volcano as I could. I could feel the heat pumping from inside the volcano. Now, I know what you're probably thinking. The Nether is hot, and it has a lot of lava everywhere. But, hey, we don't swim in the stuff, you know.

I held Melvin firmly in my hand, then I pulled my arm back and threw him as hard as I could. He shot through the air, headed straight for the volcano mouth and plummeted inside. Next thing you know, he was totally out of sight.

I breathed a sigh of relief, even though I could hear a faint but really creepy laugh in the background.

Eh. . .who cares. Melvin the Taboo Tiki idol that had plagued my entire vacation was gone.

I scurried back to the railings, and Lucy helped me climbed through to safety. All of a sudden, as we started walking back toward the hut to join Mr. and Mrs. Lurker, something strange started happening. Then me and Lucy turned around.

"What the what?!!"

The lava started bubbling, and spurting and rising. Then. . .

BOOOOM!!!!

The lava started spewing out of the mouth of the volcano.

Next thing you know, everybody in the hut started yelling and screaming and running for their lives.

Then the lava started rising and flowing down the side of the volcano toward the town.

Mr. and Mrs. Lurker came running from the hut and screamed for us to get on the bus.

I was about to get out of there when I realized what I needed to do.

"I can't!" I cried. "This is my fault."

"How can a volcano erupting be your fault?" Mrs. Lurker asked. "Don't be ridiculous, Herobrine. Come quickly."

Mr. Lurker gave me a look that said, 'Yeah, it was probably all your fault.'

"I have to stop this!" I said.

Mr. Lurker then threw Lucy into the bus. Everybody screeched away and rocketed down the mountainside as quickly as they could.

I wanted to run back over to the mouth of the volcano and get Melvin back, but there was no way I could do that now.

Suddenly, the volcano spit out a fountain of lava high into the air. And as I looked down at the town, I realized the lava was almost halfway there.

As I looked at the lava slowly creeping toward the town, I got an idea.

The only way to stop the lava was to dig a huge trench that would lead the lava away from the town and into the sea. So, I ran down the road as fast as I could. And since the lava was moving really slow—I knew I could outrun it.

After a few minutes, I was ahead of the lava and moving quickly toward the town. But, when I got to the town, everybody was in a panic.

"A shovel! I need a shovel!" I cried.

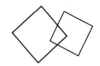

But nobody paid attention. They were too busy running for their lives.

I saw a gardening shop with a load of shovels and rakes on the porch. I grabbed the largest shovel I could find and sprinted back up the mountain. I plunged the shovel into the ground as the lava flowed toward me.

I dug with all the speed I could, but it wasn't fast enough.

Oh man! I have to do something! I have to do something!

Suddenly, out of nowhere, a surge of energy shot through my body. . .kinda like when I put my head in the microwave at Lucy's house. And it filled my body starting from my feet, through my legs, through my chest and, finally, through my head.

Then, I started floating in the air! I looked at the lava as it was just about to hit the town. So, I focused all my energy on the trench, clenched my butt cheeks and then. . .

KABABOOOOOMM!!!!

A blast of white light shot out of my eyeballs and blasted the trench wide open. Then I started floating all the way to the edge of the island blasting the ground on my way. Finally, I reached the edge of the island, but a huge boulder was blocking the way.

I clenched my butt cheeks tight enough to crack a walnut, then. . .

BABLAMMM!

I blew the boulder into little pieces.

I turned around, and the lava was flowing through the trench and out to the sea.

I used my last bit of energy to float back to town and then I collapsed on the ground.

Lucy and Mr. and Mrs. Lurker ran over to me.

"Are you OK?" Lucy asked me.

"Yeah, I'm good," I said, exhausted.

Suddenly, there was a massive explosion from the volcano and a huge eruption of lava spewed into the air. Then, I saw something hurtling down toward us. It came from the explosion and was dropping fast.

We all stepped back, crouched low, and covered our heads. Then, the object hit the ground and rolled to within an inch of my feet. I looked over at it.

It was Melvin.

"Wow, Melvin is so nasty that not even the volcano wanted him," Lucy said.

But, when we looked at Melvin, his creepy smile had disappeared. Now he just looked like he had a big pout on his face.

Meanwhile, the lava slowly stopped flowing and the volcano gradually calmed down until it returned to normal.

When Melvin had cooled down, the old man from the Volcano Store came by and picked him up.

"This idol is now clean," the old man said. "You have exorcised the demon."

Crowds began to form around me, and soon everyone started to cheer and clap.

"You saved the day, Herobrine!" Lucy said. "You saved the town from the volcano. You're a hero!"

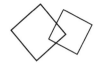

I tried to crack a smile and wave, hoping that no one would find out that I was the one who started it in the first place.

Later, we climbed back into the bus and drove away from the town as the night stars flickered above us.

As we left, the last face I saw was that of the old man. He waved at us, and when we were far enough away he gave Melvin to a tourist for a couple of bucks, put the money in his pocket and just walked away.

Chapter 14
The Trip Home

All the activity at the volcano had worn me out and I had the best night's sleep that I'd had since we arrived in Hawaii.

Now it was morning, and we were about to catch the arrow-plane home. It was the crack of dawn and we got up and packed our bags. I put in my shorts, towels, speedos, and all the Hawaiian shirts I made that I didn't even get a chance to wear.

We dragged our cases down to the main hotel reception, then we got on the bus and headed off to the airport. It was only a short trip, but Mr. and Mrs. Lurker and Lucy all fell asleep the moment we pulled away from the hotel entrance.

When we got to the arrow-port I I knew where to go and where all the portals were. However, I got stuck walking through the big metal portal, again.

But once through, Lucy and I raced to a Hawaiian store to get some stuff to take home with us.

Behind the counter was an old man who looked just like the old man from the Volcano Store.

"Hey, aren't you the man from the Volcano Store?" Lucy asked him.

"Naw, that's my brother Kai. My name is Keanu," he said.

Then Lucy poked me in the ribs as she pointed to the wall. When I looked up there was an entire rack full of Melvin Tiki idols.

"What the what?!!!"

"You like those?" Keanu asked. "They're one of kind. They bring good luck. Only $9.99 please."

"Uh. . .no. . .we're OK," Lucy said.

"How much is that one?" I asked, pointing to the real cool looking doll in the wooden coffin.

"Special price. Twenty dollars, just for you," Keanu said.

"I'll take it!"

Lucy just gave me that look again.

"What? It'll remind me of my first vacation in Hawaii," I said.

Lucy just smacked herself in the forehead.

I don't know what the big deal was.

It was only a doll.

The End

Leave Us a Review

Please support us by leaving a review. The more reviews we get the more books we will write!

And if you really liked this book, please tell a friend. I'm sure they will be happy you told them about it.

Check Out Our Other Books from Zack Zombie Publishing

The Diary of a Minecraft Zombie
Book Series

*Get The Entire Series on
Amazon Today!*

The Ultimate Minecraft Comic Book Series

*Get the Entire Series on
Amazon Today!*

Herobrine's Wacky Adventures

Get The Entire Series on Amazon Today!

The Mobbit

An Unexpected Minecraft Journey

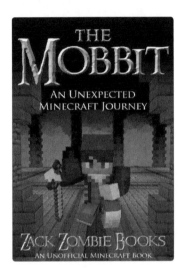

Get The Entire Series On Amazon Today!

Minecraft
Galaxy Wars

*Get The Entire Series on
Amazon Today!*

Ultimate Minecraft Secrets:

An Unofficial Guide to Minecraft Tips, Tricks and Hints to Help You Master Minecraft

Get Your Copy on Amazon Today!

Made in the USA
Middletown, DE
18 September 2017